BIG
BEASTS

Kangaroo

Stephanie Turnbull

Published by Smart Apple Media,
an imprint of Black Rabbit Books
P.O. Box 3263, Mankato, Minnesota, 56002
www.blackrabbitbooks.com

Designed by Hel James
Edited by Mary-Jane Wilkins

Library of Congress Cataloging-in-Publication Data
Turnbull, Stephanie.
 Kangaroo / Stephanie Turnbull.
    pages cm -- (Big beasts)
 Summary: "Describes the characteristics of Kangaroos
and their life and habitat"-- Provided by publisher.
 Audience: K to Grade 3.
 Includes index.
 ISBN 978-1-62588-166-3
1. Kangaroos--Juvenile literature. I. Title.
 QL737.M35T87 2015
 599.2'2--dc23
                        2014003969

Photo acknowledgements
l = left, r = right, t = top, b = bottom
title page Smileus/Shutterstock; 3 Volodymyr Burdiak/
Shutterstock; 4 Eric Isselee/Shutterstock; 5 iStock/Thinkstock;
6 Curioso, 7 Katarina Christenson/both Shutterstock; 8 mark
higgins; 9 Janelle Lugge/both Shutterstock; 10 iStock/Thinkstock;
11 Christopher Meder/Shutterstock; 12 Christoffer Hansen Vika;
13 Bernhard Richter/both Shutterstock; 14 dmvphotos;
15 mark higgins/both Shutterstock; 16 iStock/Thinkstock;
17 electra/Shutterstock; 18 Chris Howey; 19 Kjuuurs/
both Shutterstock; 20 iStock; 21 Hemera/both Thinkstock;
22 iStock/Thinkstock; 23 John Carnemolla/Shutterstock
Cover Smileus/Shutterstock

Printed in China

DAD0059
032014
9 8 7 6 5 4 3 2 1

Contents

Kangaroos are **massive!**

Giant Jumpers

Kangaroos are tall, fast-moving marsupials from Australia.

They have powerful back legs, huge feet, and a long, strong tail.

Kangaroos are the only large animals that get around by hopping.

Reds **and Grays**

The biggest kangaroos
of all are red kangaroos.
They live in central
Australia—one of
the hottest, driest
places on Earth.

Gray kangaroos are shorter and heavier. They live in eastern, western, and southern Australia, where more grass grows.

Spring Loaded

Kangaroos take huge leaps with no effort at all.

Their back legs work just like springs. Kangaroos push off with both feet together, bounce forward, land... then *boing* right up again.

They can hop a long way
without getting tired.

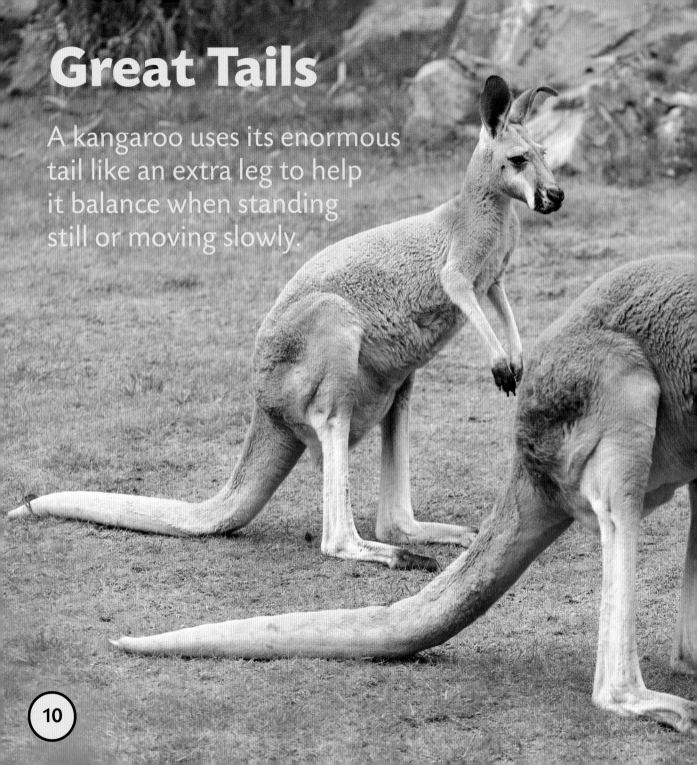

Great Tails

A kangaroo uses its enormous tail like an extra leg to help it balance when standing still or moving slowly.

10

A kangaroo's tail also gives it an extra *push* to hop, then sticks out as it soars gracefully through the air.

Lazy Days

Kangaroos spend most of the day resting under shady trees, out of the baking sun. They lick their arms to keep cool.

In the early morning and late afternoon, when the sun is less strong, they graze on grass or small bushes.

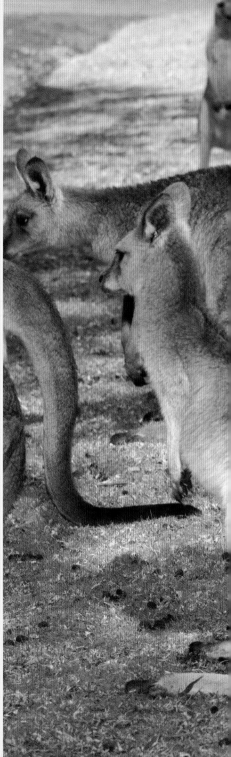

Friendly Mobs

Kangaroos don't like to be alone.
They live in groups called mobs.

Mobs of kangaroos live wherever
there is plenty of grass to eat.
Some even live on golf courses!

They communicate with grunts,
clicks, sniffs, and nose touching.

Bouncy Babies

Baby kangaroos, called joeys, are born blind, hairless and the size of a grape.

At first a joey stays in its mother's pouch, drinking her milk, until it grows furry and strong.

Soon the joey is ready to climb out of the pouch and take its first hops.

Let's Fight

Kangaroos aren't fierce animals, but sometimes young males fight over who's the most important.

First, they stand as tall as they can.

Then they *swat* each other, lock arms and **wrestle**. They even balance on their tails to give a mighty **kick**.

Danger!

Kangaroos swivel their long ears to pick up sounds.

If they hear danger, they thump their feet to warn their mob.

Most animals leave adult kangaroos alone, but wild dogs called dingoes may attack joeys.

Cars often scare kangaroos.
Signs warn people to drive carefully nearby.

BIG Facts

The biggest red kangaroos tower over an adult human.

Kangaroo mobs can be **huge**. As many as 1,500 kangaroos may gather in good eating spots.

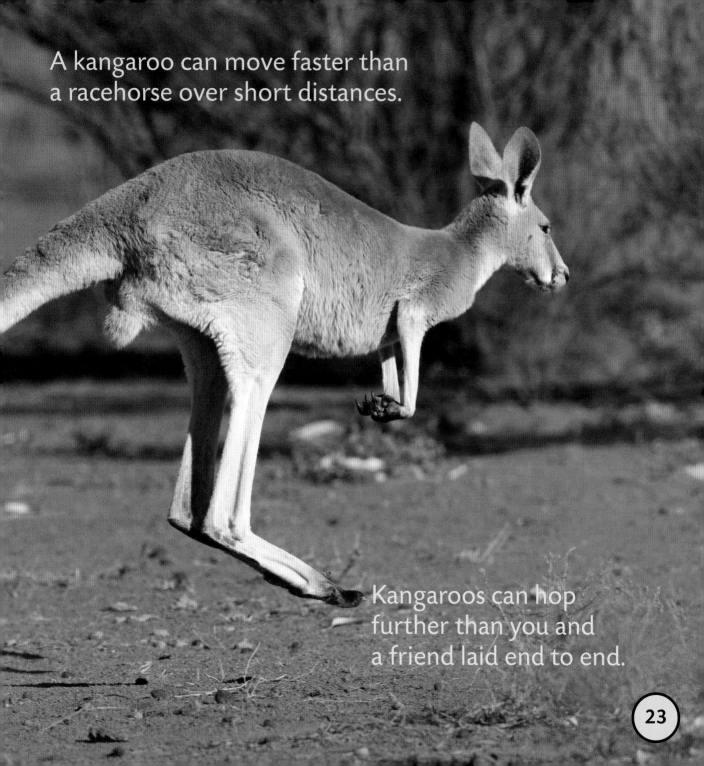

A kangaroo can move faster than a racehorse over short distances.

Kangaroos can hop further than you and a friend laid end to end.

23

Useful Words

graze
To feed on grass.

joey
A baby kangaroo. Usually just one joey is born at once.

marsupial
A type of furry animal that carries its babies in a pouch.

pouch
A fold of skin on a female kangaroo where babies live.

Index

Web Link

Visit this web site for great kangaroo facts:
www.nationalgeographic.co.uk/kids/animals/
creaturefeature/kangaroos

24